LET'S START
RIVER PIKE
FISHING

Richard Willett

The Crowood Press

First published in 1990 by
The Crowood Press
Ramsbury, Marlborough,
Wiltshire SN8 2HE

British Library Cataloguing in Publication Data

Willett, Richard
    River pike fishing.
    1. Pike. Angling. Manuals
    I. Title
    799.1'753

    ISBN 1–85223–310–9

Typeset by Jahweh Associates. Stroud
Printed in Great Britain by MacLehose & Partners Ltd

Contents

4

Pike

Pike have long been the subject matter of myths and folklore; they are also subject to more misconceptions than any other species. The stories of pike which attack and slaughter anything from ducks to dogs are endless. Most of these stories have no truth in them whatsoever.

The pike is a large predatory fish which feeds by charging into a shoal of fish and seizing the one that is the slowest in dashing out of its way. It is beautifully streamlined, with a large tail and with the dorsal fin placed far back along its body. It has a tremendous turn of speed from being stationary, but will seldom chase prey over long distances.

The pike's extremely large flattened mouth and sharp teeth are perfect for seizing hold of fish. Its teeth are hinged to fold back towards its throat, so it is a one-way trip for any prey. Pike usually grab their prey across the middle and turn it to swallow it head first.

As soon as the head of a fish enters the predator's throat, very strong digestive juices begin to work. When a pike tackles large prey, the head of the victim will be partly digested whilst the tail will still be sticking out of the pike's mouth. Pike will also drag down small ducklings paddling across the water and eat them.

The eyes on a pike are situated near the top of its head so it can observe the water above more easily than the water below. Therefore, surface feeders are more likely to be noticed than mid-water feeders.

The distribution of pike is widespread in both Britain and Europe. Often they are the only species of coarse fish to inhabit fast-flowing, cold, game rivers. In this case, where the pike's prey is limited to trout and salmon, pike can grow to very large proportions. In suitable waters they can grow to a weight of around fifty pounds. The average size of a pike is well below this weight and in many waters a pike weighing more than fifteen pounds is a good fish.

Pike spawn very early in the year, well before other species of coarse fish. By the time the fry of other species have hatched and are shoaled in vast numbers, the tiny pike will have grown enough to eat them. Pike are solitary fish that are widely distributed in rivers, but concentrations of them will occur in favoured areas. It is no coincidence that where there are vast numbers of other species of fish to feed on, large pike can be found.

Location

Pike will frequently patrol the edges of weed beds or the vicinity of submerged branches or floating debris in rivers. Occasionally they will feed frantically and locating them is easy. A pike charging into a shoal of small roach or dace feeding close to the surface will cause them to scatter in panic and they will often leap clean out of the water.

Anglers continually hooking and landing small fish may find a pike will come along and grab hold of a hooked fish, attracted by its struggle and distress. Fish held in keepnets are a big attraction for the pike. It is not at all unusual to look down at your net and

Locating pike.

Undercuts – a good place to put a bait or lure. Float fish or sink and draw.

Reed beds on the far bank – plenty of cover from reeds and trees. A bait such as sprat or roach can be trotted along or fished sink and draw. Always a good area to locate pike.

Open water – watch signs mean pike ar bait.

see a pike lying with its snout pressed against the mesh. A pike will even grab hold of a net and shake it frantically in an effort to get at the fish inside.

Pike that behave in this way are extremely easy to catch. Mount a live or deadbait on a wire trace and gently lower it into the water, in the position that you saw the pike. You won't have long to wait before the predator appears to snap up your bait. Do not delay the strike as the pike will turn and swallow the fish in one move. If the water is clear you might be able to watch the pike puffing its gills out as it swallows your bait.

...vity of other fish. Frantic
Fish a lure or float fish a

A bait or a lure worked along the nearside reed bed will bring good results.

Lilies – pike will lie in wait here.

Sink and Draw Deadbaiting

Sink and draw is the simplest form of deadbaiting, and is one of the most effective and exciting. Some anglers think that deadbaiting is a static, boring and inactive process of fishing, but sink and draw can be a very absorbing method of catching pike.

Use a wire trace and basic snap tackle as shown. Make sure the wire is flexible so that the bait is presented in a natural manner, as otherwise the bait will be ignored or rejected.

The length of the wire trace should not be less than 20 inches. When using small fish baits such as gudgeon or roach use a single treble hook fastened to the end of the wire trace, or a large single hook. A swivel should be fastened to the other end of the trace to which the reel line should be tied using a clinch knot. The number of hooks you fasten

double-hook rig

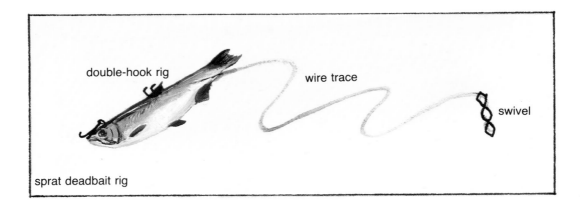

double-hook rig

wire trace

swivel

sprat deadbait rig

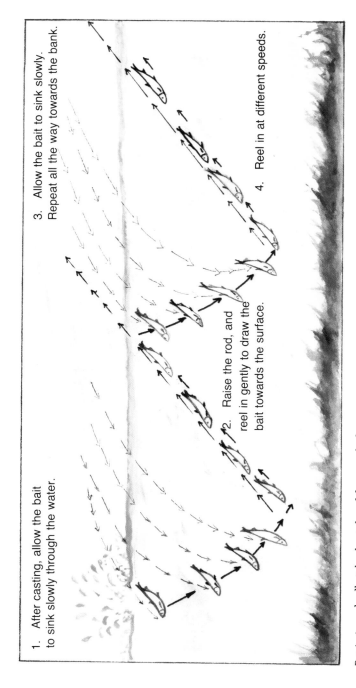

1. After casting, allow the bait to sink slowly through the water.

2. Raise the rod, and reel in gently to draw the bait towards the surface.

3. Allow the bait to sink slowly. Repeat all the way towards the bank.

4. Reel in at different speeds.

Retrieving a deadbait by the sink and draw method.

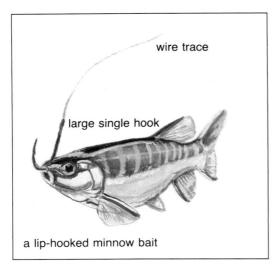

wire trace

large single hook

a lip-hooked minnow bait

into which a firm hookhold must be made from the strike. If you use a large deadbait, two treble hooks are needed as this will ensure a better hookhold when you strike. A small fish such as a roach or dace will be engulfed immediately so a small treble or single hook will be enough to hold on the strike.

For repeated casting and retrieving of a deadbait it is best to use small- to medium-sized baits. The larger the bait the stronger your tackle needs to be. Always ensure that the swim-bladder of the bait fish is punctured before using it, as otherwise it will float. This can be done by sticking a baiting needle along the body of the fish at intervals.

to the trace or the decision to use a large single hook or a combination of the two depends on the size of the deadbait you are using.

Pike have extremely hard mouths

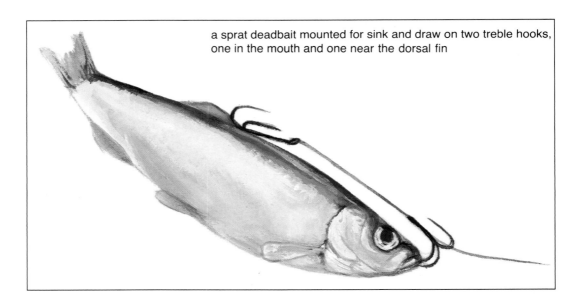

a sprat deadbait mounted for sink and draw on two treble hooks, one in the mouth and one near the dorsal fin

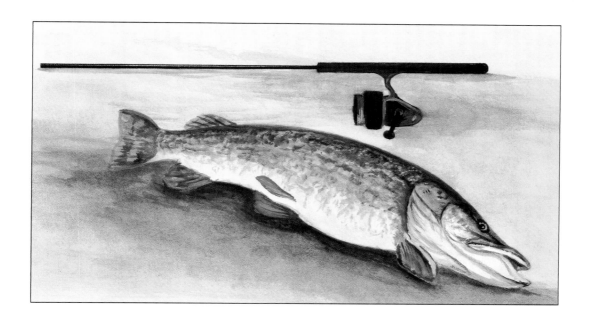

Sprats are an extremely soft bait so, to prevent them from falling off the hook during casting, it is best to mount them on two small treble hooks set a couple of inches apart. Stick a point of the first treble into the mouth of the sprat and a point of the second treble into its back next to the dorsal fin.

No leads or floats are needed for this method of sink and draw. The bait fish is cast out into the swim and then allowed to flutter down through the water enticingly. Very often a pike will grab the fish as it sinks slowly through the water.

If no bites occur, allow the bait to rest on the bottom for a few minutes, then raise the rod tip and reel in slowly to lift the bait up through the water. Repeat the process till you eventually draw the bait back to the swim you are fishing. The idea is to imitate a wounded or sick fish, keeping the bait constantly moving by fluttering it up and down. Few pike can resist a bait fished in this way.

Once the bait is picked up by a pike don't delay the strike. To make sure you drive the hooks home properly, tighten up the line, sweeping the rod back in a smooth powerful action. Do not make a hasty snatch.

When fishing a deadbait sink and draw you can cover many likely-looking swims. If no bites occur after about a dozen retrieves, move on to another swim and try again. This is a very roving and enjoyable method of catching pike and is also very successful.

Float Fishing

This method of river pike fishing is done in much the same way as fishing for chub. The plan is to search the swim either close in or across at the far bank.

With this float rig it is possible to search the swim you are fishing. Lines of between 10 and 15 pounds' breaking strain will cope with most river fishing. I regularly use 11-pound BS. I also check the line regularly for abrasions, ensuring that it is always in top condition.

My method for river pike fishing requires the float fixed in position. I attach it via a link swivel at the bottom, and the line is passed through a large rubber sleeve at the top. This set-up also makes changing floats very easy. To prevent the float creeping down the line when holding back, I tie in a stop knot above and below the slider.

fix crimp with pliers

making a trace

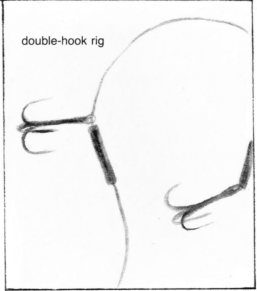

double-hook rig

The weight size is also an important factor, so check your float and the size of your bait to sort this out. It will usually be about ½ to 1 ounce in weight.

Reliable pike traces can be bought ready-made from your local tackle shop. Never tie hooks direct to nylon when pike fishing. The result will be dead pike. The finished trace should be about 20 inches long. The distance between the two hooks is variable depending on the size of the bait, but 3 to 4 inches is fine in most cases.

Hook size should be about 8 or 10 and barbless treble. The bait is hooked

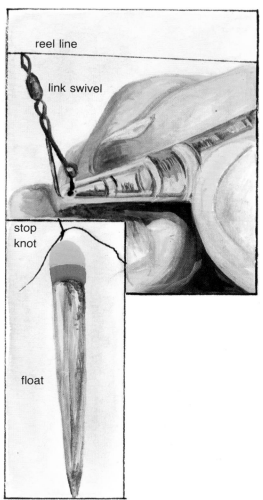

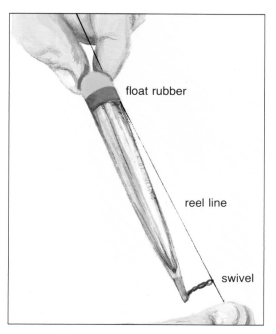

head first in the top lip, and the bottom treble fixed just under the dorsal fin.

The method is a roving one so you don't need a lot of equipment. Store all your equipment in a rucksack and keep it on your back. The large landing-net is propped up against your side while working the bait through the swim.

working a bait along the river

paying out line

Line is fed from the spool as in conventional trotting methods, the float being held back or allowed to run through at the pace allowed by the current and the paternoster weight.

Pike are easy to unhook providing you have the right tools for the job. A pair of long forceps will deal with all but the most deeply hooked pike. A Drennan disgorger will save a deeply hooked pike, but in most cases you should not need it.

Do not leave runs – strike immediately! Also, if you always use barbless trebles you will never have unhooking problems.

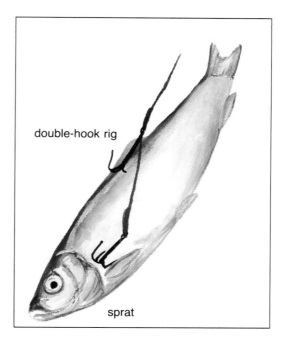

double-hook rig

sprat

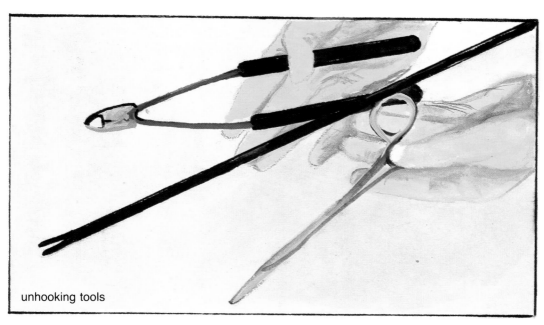

unhooking tools

Lure Fishing

A plug, spinner or spoon is an artificial lure, usually made of wood, plastic or metal, and is most often designed to look something like a fish.

Plugs can be classified in various ways; some are built to resemble fish and their action is supposed to be close to that of a healthy or injured fish, while others have little resemblance to a fish but have an action, usually vibrant, which alone is attractive to the attentions of a pike.

They can also be classified by the manner in which they are retrieved through the water. Some float or splash on the surface, some others float on the surface but dive to various depths when retrieved, while others sink at different speeds and can be returned to the rod in different ways.

When spinning for pike, use large Mepps or kidney spoons. Special short rods called 'Baitcasters' can be used in conjunction with a closed-face spinning reel or multiplier and make an enjoyable way of catching pike. Otherwise, a 10-foot carp rod and fixed

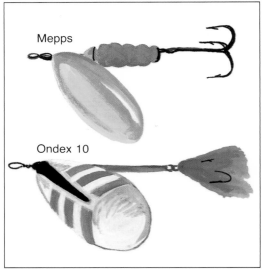

Mepps

Ondex 10

spool reel will do the trick. To prevent your line kinking as the spinner revolves, tie a swivel into your line a short distance away from the spinner or plug. Spinners themselves are attached to a swivel but this is often not enough to prevent line kink.

When spinning, always try to vary the speed of the retrieve. Reel in in a series of quick turns, then slow right down. This will cause the spinner to rise and

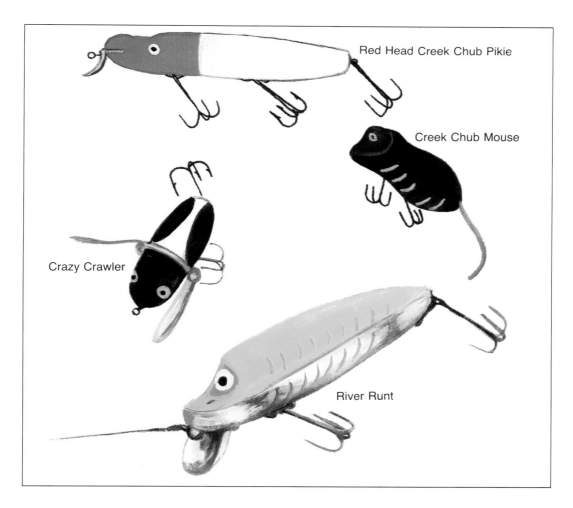

Red Head Creek Chub Pikie

Creek Chub Mouse

Crazy Crawler

River Runt

fall in the water in a very exciting way. Do not reel in too fast and do not lift the spinner out until it is right into the bank as a pike will often follow a spinner right up to the bank and grab it at the last moment.

Plugs are used very successfully in weedy water when fishing for pike and the same tackle can be used as is used for spinning. Plug fishing is similar to spinning except that the plug either floats or dives. On the front of some plugs there are spoon-shaped vanes of various sizes – the larger the vane the deeper the plug will dive. The vane causes the plug to dive as it is reeled in, and the motion of the plug as it dives makes it look exactly like an injured fish to the pike. This method of pike fishing is very exciting and mobile.

Knots

Three-turn Loop knot.

Method of joining hook length to reel line.

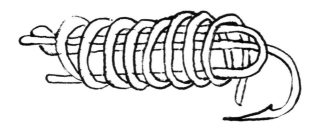

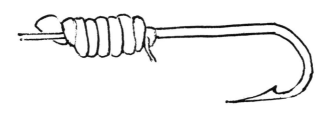

Spade End knot.

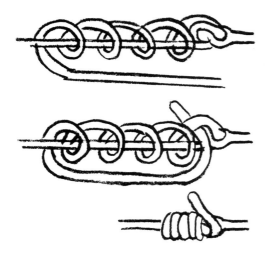

Clinch knot.

Playing and Landing

On hooking a fish, especially a large one, keep the tip of the rod well up and maintain a steady pressure. Never point the rod at the fish. The clutch on the reel must be adjusted prior to fishing so that it yields line when the pressure on it is just below the line's breaking strain.

If a hooked fish makes for an area where underwater snags exist, it can be turned by applying side-strain.

Have the net close at hand. When the fish shows signs of tiring, slip the net into the water and keep it stationary. Never jab at the fish in an attempt to scoop it out. Bring the fish over the awaiting net, not the net to the fish.

Handling and Hook Removal

Always make sure your hands are wet before handling a fish. Grip the fish firmly but gently just behind the gill covers. The jaw will automatically open – don't use gags.

If the hook is lightly embedded near the front of the mouth, it is possible to remove it with the fingertips; otherwise, use a disgorger.

With larger fish, it is best to leave them lying in the damp net while you remove the hook. Artery forceps are best for this. When they are locked, a really good grip is maintained on the hook, which can be gently eased out. A damp towel positioned between the hand and the fish is advisable, as the larger fish are very strong and need some holding if they suddenly decide to leap about.

unhooking a pike

Retaining and Returning Fish

Fish should only be retained in a large knotless keepnet, which is well covered by water, preferably in a shaded area. Never keep them for any length of time; in fact, there is no point in retaining them at all unless they are to be weighed or photographed at the end of your fishing session. Pike are best retained in keepsacks where they will lie quietly.

Never throw a fish into a net, but place it in gently using wet hands.

When returning fish, gently gather up the net until the area occupied by the fish is reached; place the mouth of the net underwater and allow the fish to swim off.

A large fish should be held underwater in an upright position with both hands until it swims away.

Index